D0269597

Eclipse of the Sun

Written by Steve Parker
Illustrated by Michael Posen

First published in 1999 by Parragon

Parragon
Queen Street House
4 Queen Street
Bath BA1 1HE

ISBN 0-75253-282-0

Printed in Italy

Produced by
Monkey Puzzle Media Ltd
Gissing's Farm
Fressingfield
Suffolk IP21 5SH

Designer: Victoria Webb
Editor: Stephen Setford
Artwork commissioning: Roger Goddard-Coote
Project manager: Alex Edmonds

Contents

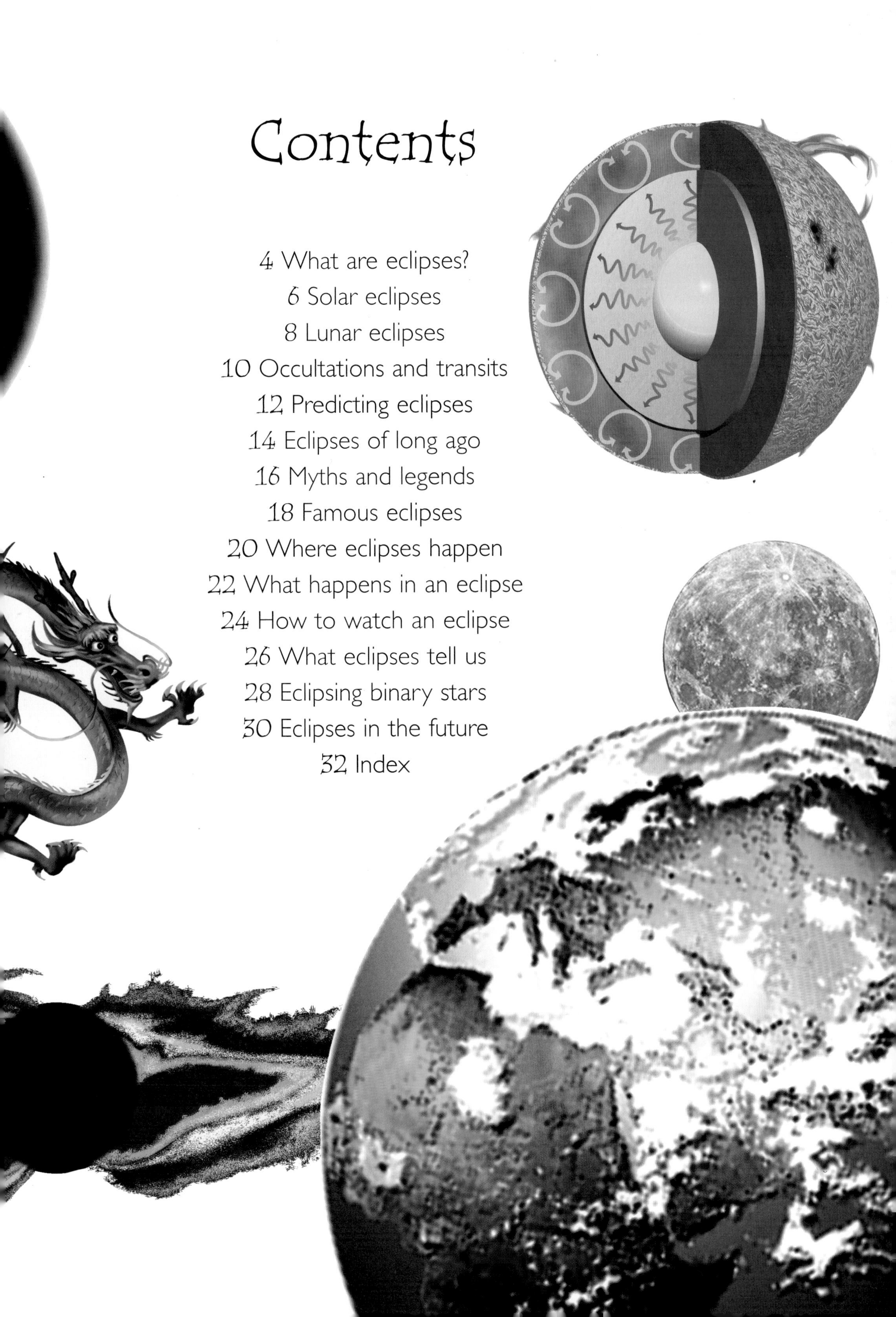

In a solar eclipse, the Moon passes between the Sun and the Earth.

How can a horse win an eclipse?
Because the Eclipse Award is the name of a presentation each year to the best racehorse in the USA. The mega-famous, record-breaking horse Secretariat won this award two years running, 1972 and 1973.

What is a solar eclipse?

IT'S WHEN THE MOON PASSES BETWEEN THE SUN AND OUR PLANET, EARTH. ("Solar" means something to do with the Sun.) The Sun, Moon and Earth are all zooming through space, on their well-known paths. Now and again they come into line. If the Moon is in the middle, it gets between us here on Earth, and the Sun. The Earth is in the shadow of the Moon. The Sun looks as if it "goes out" as the Moon passes in front of it. But a solar eclipse lasts only a few minutes. The Moon moves on, the Sun appears again, and all is well.

The Moon moves in front of the Sun and stops some or all of its light from reaching the Earth.

How can the Moon cover the Sun when it is so small?
Because the Moon is so much nearer. The Moon is about 3,475 km (2,155 miles) across and 385,000 km (240,000 miles) away. The Sun is about 1.39 million km (0.86 million miles) across and 150 million km (93 million miles) away. So the Sun is around 400 times wider than the Moon – but almost 400 times farther away. This is why, from Earth, they look the same size.

Have there always been eclipses?
Yes. Well, not "always". Only for about 4.5 billion years! This was the time when the Sun, Earth and Moon formed, along with all the other planets, and their moons too – in fact, when the whole solar system formed. The Earth and Moon have been following their paths or orbits ever since, and eclipses have been happening.

What does a solar eclipse look like?
Seen from Earth, it looks like a giant black disc passing across the Sun. The dark disc is the Moon. Since the Sun's light and warmth can't pass through the Moon, it is blocked off from reaching Earth. So here on Earth, it seems as if the Sun has gone out. It goes dark and cool – almost like night-time.

How can a man win an eclipse?

Because the Special Eclipse Award is given to the very best jockeys who ride racehorses in the USA. In 1994 the jockey Eddie Arcaro received a Special Eclipse Award from the Thoroughbred Racing Association. He had ridden 4,779 winning horses in a career of more than 24,000 races lasting 30 years.

How did the Ancient Romans eclipse the Ancient Greeks?

The word "eclipse" has several uses, apart from talking about solar and lunar eclipses. In general, it means to overshadow, take over, cover up, blot out, dominate or replace. In ancient times, the Roman Empire gradually conquered and took over the Greek civilization. We could say that the Romans eclipsed the Greeks.

Do owls hoot and bats fly during a solar eclipse?

Yes, sometimes. Daylight is very important to animals. Every evening, as it goes dark, the daytime animals settle down to sleep, and the night-time ones come out. A solar eclipse is like night-time, so the animals do what they'd normally do at dusk. They don't know the real time of day – they don't have clocks!

Do the stars come out during a solar eclipse?

Yes, if there are no clouds and the sky is clear! The stars begin to twinkle, just as they do on a clear evening as the sun sets. In fact, the stars are in the sky all the time, day and night. But during the day, the Sun is so bright, and the stars are so dim in comparison, that the Sun far outshines them. It swamps their tiny dots of light with its own massively powerful rays.

What is a lunar eclipse?

It's when the Earth passes between the Sun and the Moon. ("Lunar" means something to do with the Moon.) It happens in the same way as a solar eclipse, when the Sun, Earth and Moon come into line. But this time the Earth is in the middle. This means the Earth prevents the Sun's light from reaching the Moon. So the Moon – which shines only because it reflects, or bounces back, the Sun's light – goes dark. It's in the Earth's shadow. Like a solar eclipse, the lunar eclipse is soon over. The Earth moves on, out of the way, and the Sun's light makes the Moon shine again.

Could the Sun go out during an eclipse?

NO. DURING A SOLAR ECLIPSE, IT MAY SEEM THAT THE SUN HAS BEEN turned off, like a stellar electric light-bulb on a cosmic dimmer-switch. But the Sun is only hidden behind the Moon. It's still shining. The Sun will continue to shine for billions of years to come.

In a lunar eclipse, the Earth passes between the Sun and the Moon.

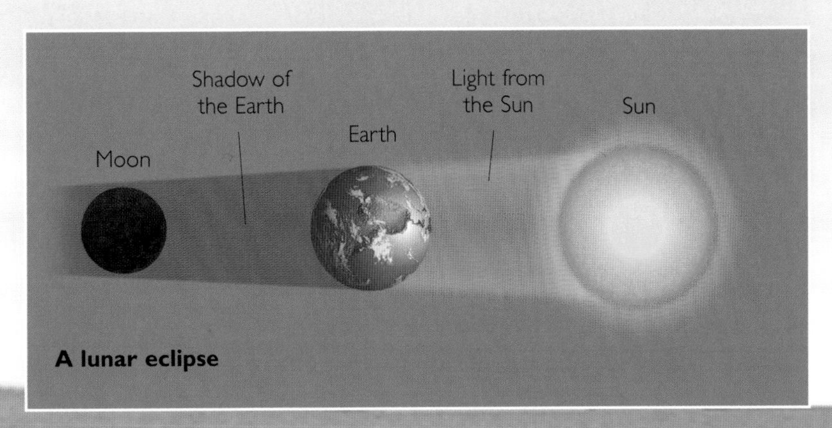

A lunar eclipse

What is a total solar eclipse?

AT SOME STAGE DURING THE ECLIPSE, THE MOON COVERS THE SUN totally. This happens when the Sun, Moon and Earth are exactly in line. The time of total coverage occurs in the middle of the eclipse, after the Moon has slowly crept across the Sun's disc, from one side. The period of totality is when the Moon completely covers the Sun. It usually lasts for just a few minutes. No part of the Sun's blinding yellow disc shows around the Moon's edge. Then the Moon moves on and the Sun peeps out from behind it again.

What is an umbra?
As the Sun shines on the Moon, the Moon casts a dark, cone-shaped shadow into space on the side away from the Sun. This is an umbra. Inside the umbra, you could not see the Sun at all, since the Moon is totally in the way. Here on Earth, an umbrella or sunshade casts an umbra too. To be in total shade, completely out of the Sun, you'd have to be inside the umbrella's umbra!

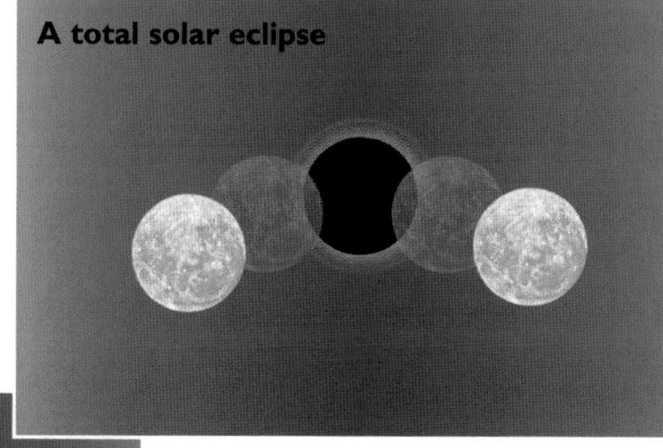

In a total eclipse of the Sun, the whole of the Sun is covered by the Moon.

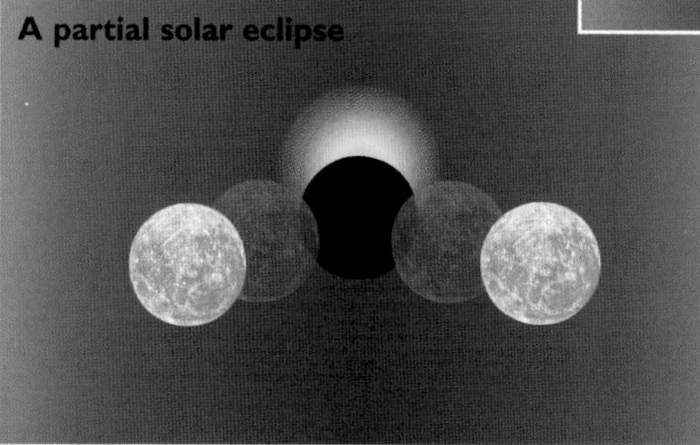

In a partial eclipse, the Moon covers only part of the Sun. Some of the Sun can be seen above or below the Moon.

An annular eclipse happens when the Moon is farthest from Earth. A bright ring can be seen around the dark disc of the Moon.

An annular solar eclipse

What is a partial solar eclipse?
When the Moon is a bit too high or low in the sky to cover the Sun completely. It covers only part of the Sun, even during the middle of the eclipse. A partial solar eclipse happens when the Sun, Moon and Earth are almost in line, but not quite. The dark disc of the Moon creeps across the bright disc of the Sun, but there is always a bit of the Sun that is not hidden, and keeps shining. So the Sun is eclipsed only partially.

What is an annular solar eclipse?
The Moon's distance from Earth varies slightly, from about 357,000 km (222,000 miles) at its nearest, to 407,000 km (253,000 miles) at its farthest. This is because the Moon goes round and round the Earth not in an exact circle, but in an oval-type shape – an ellipse. When the Moon is farthest from Earth, it looks smallest. If there is an eclipse at this time, the Moon is not quite big enough in the sky to cover the whole Sun. As the Moon passes across the middle of the Sun, the Sun's bright yellow disc is still visible around it. This forms a ring shape known as an annulus.

If the Moon was smaller, would eclipses happen?
If the Moon was smaller, its umbra would be shorter. If the Moon was about 225 km (140 miles) smaller than it is now, its umbra would be so short that it would never reach Earth. So we would never see any total solar eclipses. But we would see partial ones.

Can you see a solar eclipse when it's cloudy?
No, you cannot see the actual eclipse, because you cannot see the Sun or Moon through the clouds. But you can see the effects of the eclipse. It goes dark like a cloudy evening, then gets back to full daylight again.

Earth

Penumbra

Umbra

Moon

Sun

What is a penumbra?

Around the Moon's cone-shaped black shadow, or umbra, is another area which is partly shadow. This area is the penumbra. Inside the penumbra, there is always part of the Sun visible, so you would see a partial solar eclipse. On Earth, an umbrella or sunshade casts a penumbra too. If you see part of the Sun peeping around the edge of the umbrella, you're inside the umbrella's penumbra!

Can you see an eclipse at night?

No, because you cannot see the Sun! The Earth has spun around so that you are on the side facing away from the Sun. That is why it's night-time! However you might be able to see a lunar eclipse at night, because you can see the Moon.

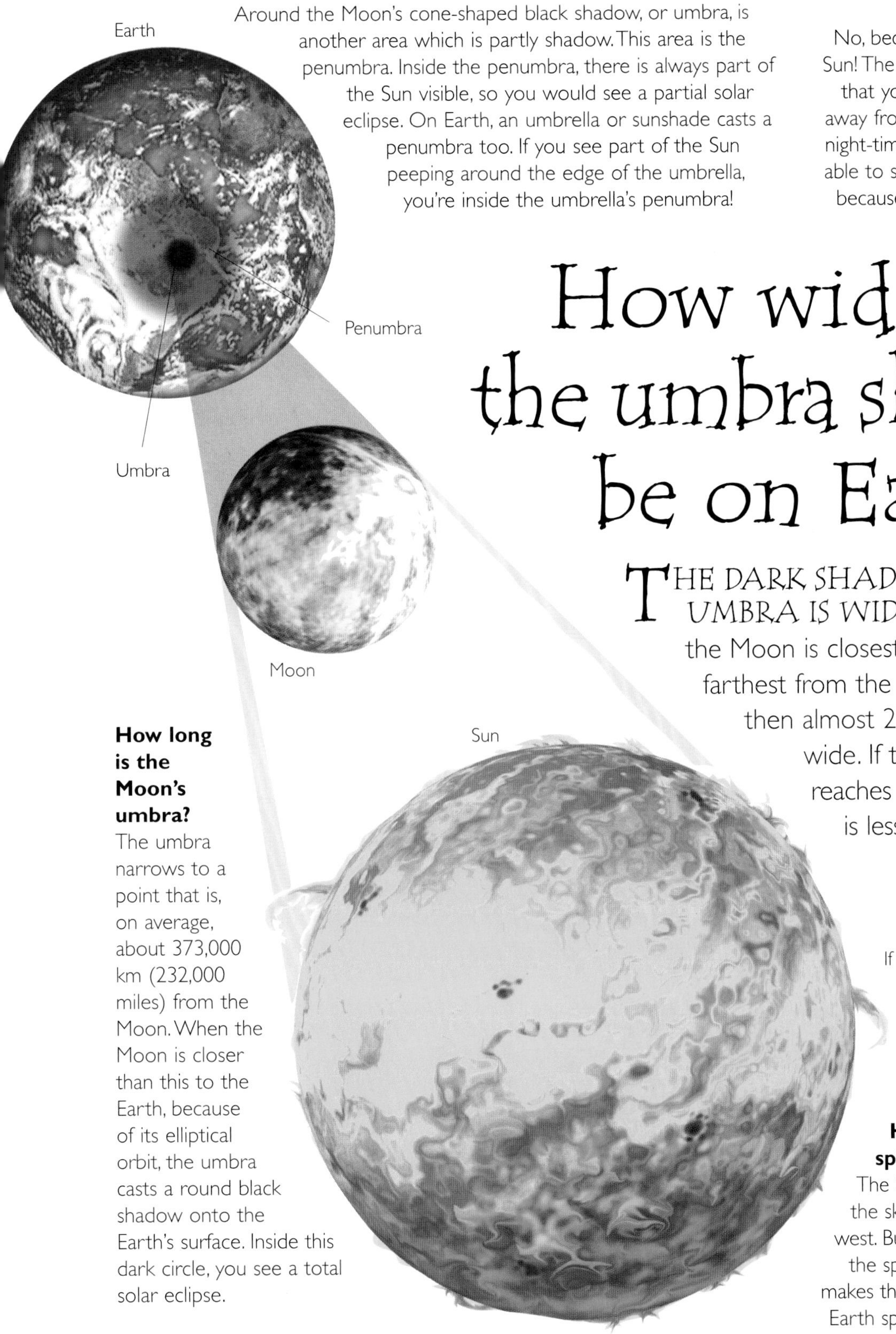

How wide can the umbra shadow be on Earth?

THE DARK SHADOW OF THE UMBRA IS WIDEST WHEN the Moon is closest to the Earth but farthest from the Sun. The shadow is then almost 270 km (168 miles) wide. If the umbra only just reaches the Earth, its shadow is less than one kilometre (0.6 mile) wide.

If you are in an area covered by the umbra, you will see a total eclipse. In the penumbra you will see a partial eclipse.

How long is the Moon's umbra?

The umbra narrows to a point that is, on average, about 373,000 km (232,000 miles) from the Moon. When the Moon is closer than this to the Earth, because of its elliptical orbit, the umbra casts a round black shadow onto the Earth's surface. Inside this dark circle, you see a total solar eclipse.

Does the umbra's length vary?

Yes. The Moon's orbit around the Earth is not a circle, but an ellipse. Likewise, the Earth orbits the Sun, and the Earth's orbit is an ellipse, too. So the distance from the Earth to the Sun varies. Since the Moon stays orbiting the Earth, the distance from the Moon to the Sun varies as well. When the Moon (with Earth) is closest to the Sun the umbra is 367,000 km (228,000 miles). When it is farthest the umbra is 379,800 km (235,000 miles).

How does the Earth's spinning affect eclipses?

The Sun appears to pass across the sky from left to right, east to west. But the Sun is really still. It's the spinning of the Earth that makes the Sun appear to move. The Earth spins around once each day, that is, every 24 hours. During a solar eclipse, the Earth's spinning means that the shadow of the Moon races across the Earth's surface. This is why eclipses pass quite quickly. However it's not quite so simple, because the Moon is moving too.

Could you see a lunar eclipse on the Moon?

YES. STANDING ON THE MOON AT THE RIGHT PLACE AND TIME, YOU could see the Earth pass in front of the Sun and blot out its light. From Earth, we see a lunar eclipse as the round shadow of the Earth advances across the Moon, gradually turning its surface dark.

What are the phases of the Moon?
The Moon seems to change shape each month. It goes from a thin, curved, right-side crescent, which is a new Moon, to the new half-Moon, to the whole white disc of the full Moon, to the old half-Moon, to the thin left-side crescent of the old Moon. Of course, the Moon itself does not change its ball shape. What we see is sunlight bouncing or reflecting off the Moon's surface. The changes or phases happen because we see the Moon's sunlit half from different angles, as it orbits the Earth. The rest of the Moon is there, but isn't lit.

Can there be an annular lunar eclipse?
No. Even when the Earth and Moon are farthest apart, then from the Moon, the Earth still looks much bigger in the sky than the Sun. The Earth is never small enough in the sky to cover only the central part of the Sun's disc. So a ring is not formed by the edge of the Sun and there cannot be an annular lunar eclipse.

How do the Moon's phases affect eclipses?
Because the Moon's phases, as seen from Earth, show the positions of the Earth, Moon and Sun. A solar eclipse can only happen during a new Moon. A new Moon is dark as seen from Earth, because its sunlit half is around the other side, facing the Sun. In other words, the Moon is between the Sun and the Earth. A lunar eclipse can only happen during a full Moon. A full Moon is almost all brightly sunlit, as seen from Earth, because the Sun is shining past the Earth onto the Moon. In other words, the Earth is between the Sun and the Moon.

How the Moon is coloured in a lunar eclipse

The Earth's atmosphere splits the Sun's light into the colours of the rainbow. Red light is bent around the Earth and falls on the Moon.

How can cloudy weather on Earth alter a lunar eclipse?
If the atmosphere is very cloudy where the Sun's rays just graze past the Earth, this prevents the light refraction described opposite. Red light rays cannot bend and shine onto the Moon. So the Moon looks almost black.

What colour does the Moon go during a lunar eclipse?
The Sun's rays of white light are a mixture of all the colours of the rainbow, known as light's colour spectrum. They are red, orange, yellow, green, blue, indigo and violet. In the Earth's atmosphere, the white sunlight is bent and split up into these colours. The bending or refraction works best with red light. These red rays shine onto the Moon and turn it a coppery-red colour.

How long can a total lunar eclipse last?

MUCH LONGER THAN A TOTAL SOLAR ECLIPSE. THIS IS BECAUSE THE Earth is much bigger in the sky than the Sun, and so it can blot out the Sun for longer. The period of totality of a lunar eclipse, when the Sun is hidden completely by the Earth, is about 104 minutes.

Moon astronauts watching a lunar eclipse

What is an occultation?

IT'S VERY SIMILAR TO AN ECLIPSE. ONE SPACE OBJECT OR CELESTIAL BODY passes in front of another, and covers or obscures it from view. In an occultation, usually the Moon does the covering, and it covers stars or planets. Imagine a dark night, when the Moon is new – a black disc in the black sky. As this new Moon moves, it covers the stars behind it. It's like a "black hole" arching through the sky, although it's not a real one.

Can eclipses happen without the Earth and Moon?
Yes. An eclipse is a general term for any object in space that moves in front of another one and blocks its view, blots it out or obscures it. We see solar eclipses as the Moon blocks the Sun from the Earth, and lunar eclipses as the Earth blocks the Sun from the Moon. But eclipses happen with other planets and moons, and other space bodies too, such as comets and stars.

Can occultations tell us about conditions on other worlds?
As a planet moves in front of a star, the starlight just touches or grazes the planet's edge before continuing to Earth. If the planet has an atmosphere (layer of gases) around it, the rays pass through this and change slightly, according to the types and amounts of gases. We detect the changes and work out what gases are in the planet's atmosphere.

Which planet's rings were discovered by an occultation?
Uranus. When Uranus passed in front of, or occulted, some stars behind it, detailed observations showed that it might have rings. But even the most powerful Earth telescopes could not quite see them. Then in 1986 the space probe Voyager 2 sped past Uranus and sent back incredible pictures of its thin, wispy rings.

The Moon occults stars in the night sky, hiding them from view.

An occultation

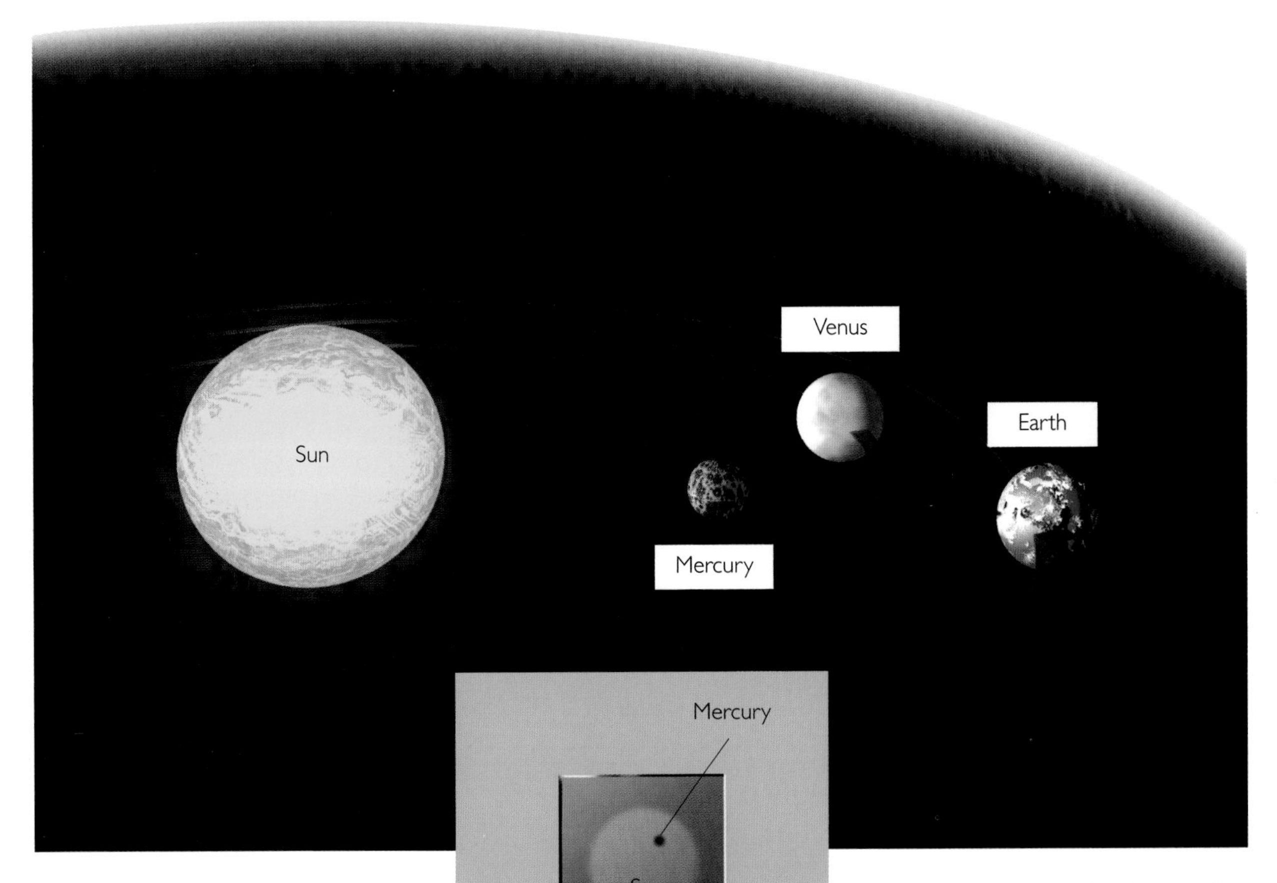

A transit of Mercury across the Sun

When Mercury passes between Earth and the Sun, we can't normally see it because Mercury is so small. If we could dim our view of the Sun, we would be able to see Mercury as a tiny black dot, as in the inset picture.

What is a transit?
It is when one space object passes across the face or disc of a larger one. This usually means the planet Mercury or Venus moving between us and the Sun. The planet looks like a tiny black dot moving across the blazing yellow disc of the Sun.

From which planet could you see Earth making a transit?
Mars would be best. This is the fourth planet away from the Sun, after Mercury, Venus and Earth. From Mars, you could see Earth as a minuscule dark spot as it passed in front of the Sun. By the time you reached the next planet out from the Sun, which is Jupiter, Earth would be too small to see easily.

Can all the planets make transits as seen from Earth?
No. Only Mercury or Venus can. This is because they are the only two planets which are closer to the Sun than we are. So they are the only two planets that can come between the Earth and Sun.

How did an occultation make a mysterious "star" visible?
Quasars are massive, mysterious objects in the depths of space. They are brighter than millions of stars, yet hardly larger than a few hundred stars. Some give out radio waves too. In the early 1960s, several quasars were detected by their radio waves, but not their light rays. In 1962 the Moon occulted the radio waves of quasar 3C-273. Astronomers could then look in the right part of the sky, and see this quasar's light.

Do other planets have eclipses?

YES, BUT VERY RARELY. MOST PLANETS HAVE THEIR OWN MOONS (only Mercury and Venus don't). A moon can pass between its planet and the Sun. But most of these moons are very small in proportion to their planet. (Our Moon is about one-quarter as wide as its planet.) So their eclipse shadows would be tiny and short, and not reach the planet's surface.

How often do eclipses happen?

THERE ARE ABOUT TWO OR THREE SOLAR ECLIPSES EACH YEAR. Some are partial, some are annular and some are total. For example, in the 10-year period from 1989 to 1999 there were 23 main solar eclipses. Eight of these were partial, seven were annular and eight were total.

What's an ecliptic, as opposed to an eclipse?

The Earth and the other planets go around the Sun in their orbits. Nearly all of these orbits are on the same level with each other in space. It's as though the Sun is on a gigantic, flat invisible table-top, with the planets rolling around it in their orbits, also on the table-top. The level, or plane, of the Earth's orbit around the Sun is called the plane of the ecliptic.

What is a node?

The Earth's orbit is at the same level or plane as the ecliptic. The level of the Moon's orbit is tilted or inclined slightly from the plane of the ecliptic. Where these two levels pass through each other, or intersect, is called a node. There are two nodes, ascending as the Moon goes above the plane or level of the ecliptic, and descending as it goes below. Eclipses can only happen when the Sun or Moon are at or very near these nodes.

A spacecraft above the Earth

Why do eclipses mean two kinds of year?

There are two kinds of year, as a result of the Sun, stars and galaxies in deep space all moving in relation to each other.

- An anomalistic year is the time taken for the Earth to make exactly one orbit around the Sun. It is 365 days 6 hours 13 minutes and 53.1 seconds. This can be thought of as a year within our solar system.
- A sidereal year is the time taken for the Sun to pass in front of, or eclipse, a particular star, to when the Sun eclipses it next time. It is 365 days 6 hours 9 minutes and 9.54 seconds. This can be thought of as a year outside the solar system, against the ever-changing background of the Universe.

How did eclipses get their name?

From the word "ecliptic". Because eclipses only happen when the Moon is on or near the ecliptic. (However, some people say it's the other way round, and the ecliptic is named after eclipses!)

Do spacecraft ever see eclipses?

Yes. Imagine a partial solar eclipse with the Moon covering the upper part of the Sun, when seen from the surface of the Earth. The Earth, Moon and Sun are not directly in line. A spacecraft like the Space Shuttle is 100–200 km (60–120 miles) above the Earth. This could make it exactly in line with the Moon and Sun. The astronauts on the spacecraft would then see a total solar eclipse. The same could happen the other way round. The astronauts might see a partial eclipse, but on the surface, you could see a total eclipse.

If a spacecraft was in the correct place, its crew would be able to see an eclipse that could not be seen from Earth.

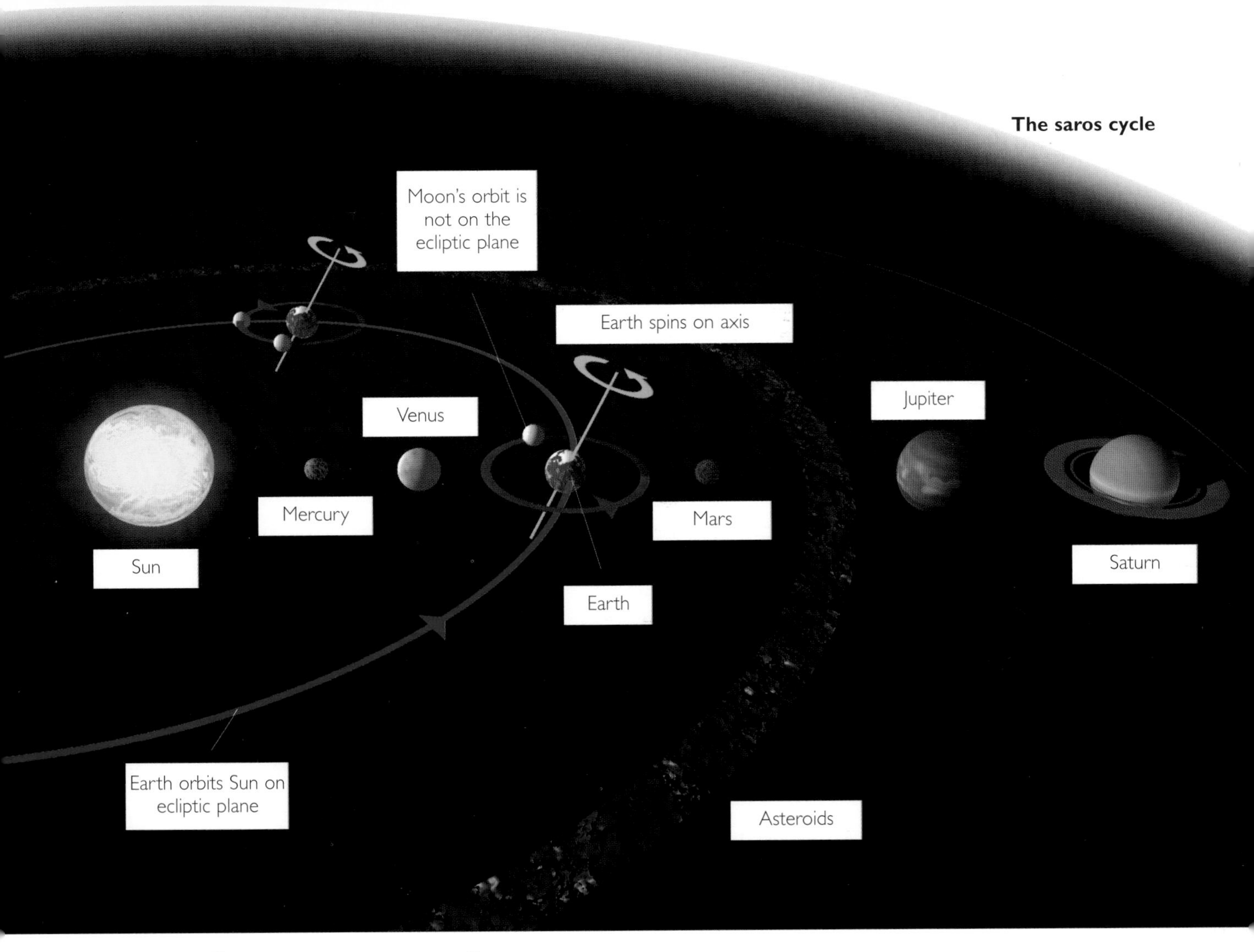

What is the saros?

Eclipses happen when the Sun and Moon are in the correct position in relation to a node.

EVERY SO OFTEN, THE SUN AND MOON COME BACK TO THE SAME POSITION in relation to one of the nodes. This means eclipses do not happen at random. They occur in a pattern, which is the result of how the Moon and Earth move on their regular orbits around the Sun. The time taken for one whole pattern or series of eclipses to occur is 6,585.3 days, that is, 18 years 11.3 days (give or take the leap year days). This time period for one whole series or pattern of eclipses is called the saros. (Saros means "repetition".) After this time, the pattern of eclipses repeats itself.

How many eclipses happen during a saros?

About 70. These are made up, on average, of 41 solar eclipses and 29 lunar eclipses. There's a maximum of seven eclipses in one year of the saros, and a minimum of two. Of the 41 or so solar eclipses that happen during a saros, about 30 or 31 are partial or annular, and the rest total. So 10 total solar eclipses happen, on average, over 18 years 11.3 days. This gives a total solar eclipse somewhere on Earth every 658 days (on average, of course).

How does the saros pattern move?

The saros means that the pattern of eclipses repeats itself, and at the same latitude on Earth – that is, at the same level north or south. But the extra one-third of a day in the saros means that the whole pattern of eclipses happens one-third of a day later in the next saros. Since the Earth turns once each day, the eclipse pattern moves about one-third of the way westwards around the globe, or 120° of longitude, each time. For example, a total solar eclipse that arcs across Europe and the Middle East will repeat itself 18 years 11.3 days later, but curve over North America, then 18 years 11.3 days later over Japan and the North-West Pacific, then 18 years 11.3 days later, back to Europe and the Middle East again.

Who first predicted an eclipse?

THE FIRST RECORDS OF ECLIPSES WERE probably made by the ancient Assyrians and Babylonians, more than 2,700 years ago. But the first person to predict an eclipse may have been Thales of Miletus, a thinker and scientist, who lived from about 625 to 546 BC. Thales calculated that a total solar eclipse would happen on 28 May in the year 585 BC. And it did. (Some experts say that this did not really happen, but the story has been told so often that now everyone believes it.)

Thales of Miletus

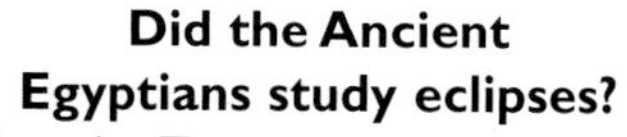

Thales may have been the first person to accurately predict an eclipse, but no one knows for certain.

Did the Ancient Egyptians study eclipses?

Not a lot. They built great pyramids and temples, worshipped many gods and spirits, invented numerous machines and gadgets, and devised various kinds of writing and mathematics. But they didn't seem interested in eclipses at all and made no proper records of them.

Who discovered the saros cycle?

As far as we know today, the astronomers of Chaldea were the first to notice that the pattern of eclipses repeated itself every 18 years and 11.3 days, which is the saros cycle (see page 13). Chaldea was a marshy region (now southern Iraq and Kuwait) that became part of Babylonia. Four great civilizations studied and reported eclipses in ancient times. Besides the Babylonians these were the Chinese, the Arabs and the Europeans. The Babylonians recorded eclipses from about the years 700 BC to AD 75.

What did the ancient world's most famous astronomer, Ptolemy, think about eclipses?

Ptolemy lived in Egypt at the time when Ancient Greece was the main power in the region. In his great book, *Almagest*, Ptolemy included reports of lunar eclipses dating back to the year 720 BC. Of course, calendars and dates were very different then. Using our modern calendar, we can work out that the first one he noted actually happened on 19 March 721 BC.

Stonehenge

Druids – the priests of the Ancient Britons – may have prayed and worshipped their gods at Stonehenge.

Who first noticed that Stonehenge was built to line up with Sun, Moon and stars?
In 1740, British history expert Dr William Stukeley noticed that some of the main stones lined up with the Sun as it rose on midsummer's day. This began the idea of Stonehenge as a great calendar-temple. In 1964 the American astronomer Gerald S Hawkins reported the results of new studies which found that Stonehenge lined up with the Sun and Moon at many other important dates and times.

What else was Stonehenge used for?
Probably lots of things. The way that Stonehenge's stones were lined up was also linked to predicting the days of midsummer and midwinter, and the days of the spring and autumn equinoxes midway between them. This would allow people to predict the seasons, know when to plant and harvest crops, and when to have their festivals, holidays and worship days. Stonehenge may have been a combination of giant calendar and temple, where druids (priests) prayed to the Sun and Moon, worshipped their gods and even made sacrifices.

Was Stonehenge built to predict eclipses?

PROBABLY AND PARTLY. THE GREAT STANDING-STONE CIRCLE monument of Stonehenge is on Salisbury Plain, in Wiltshire, England. It was built and used by Ancient Britons around 5,000 to 3,000 years ago. In the early 1960s scientists took detailed measurements of the stones' positions and fed them into a computer. They also fed in details of where the Sun, Moon and stars would have been 3,500 years ago when people used Stonehenge. They found that the stones lined up to predict both solar and lunar eclipses.

Which eclipse stopped a war?
It was the eclipse of 28 May in the year 585 BC. The Lydian people lived in the western part of Anatolia (now Turkey) in the Middle East. Led by their King Alyattes, they had been fighting the Medes from farther east for five years. The eclipse shook both armies so much that they agreed a peace deal at once.

Some Ancient Chinese people believed that an eclipse was caused by a dragon taking huge bites out of the Sun.

The dragon that ate the Sun

Which eclipse is mentioned in the Bible?

IT WAS THE ECLIPSE OF 763 BC, RECORDED BY THE ASSYRIANS. IT IS MENTIONED in the Bible in the Old Testament book of Amos, chapter 8, verse 9: " 'And it shall come to pass, in that day,' says the Lord God, 'that I will cause the sun to go down at noon, and I will darken the Earth in the clear day.' "

Who gave one of the first correct explanations of eclipses?

One of the first clear explanations of eclipses was written by Aryabhata or Aryabhatta, also known as Arjehir. He lived from about AD 475 to 550. He was born in the city of Pataliputra, now Patna, in India. He believed that the Earth spun around like a top, rather than the Sun, Moon and stars going around the Earth. In this idea, he was almost 1,000 years ahead of his time.

Who made the first accurate descriptions of eclipses?

Probably the Assyrians of Nineveh (Nineva). This city was near what is now Mosul, Iraq. They described a partial eclipse of the Sun on 15 June 763 BC. Their rivals the Babylonians conquered them but kept up the tradition of recording eclipses.

Which god caused the first eclipse by hiding in a cave?

It was a goddess, Amaterasu. Japanese legend says that she was the daughter of Izanagi, one of the fathers of the gods. Her brother, Susanoo, was very excitable and always arguing with their father. Finally, Izanagi banished his son Susanoo to a remote place. Before Susanoo left, he went to say goodbye to his sister. But he got carried away as he was bidding farewell to his old horse, and accidentally pulled off all its skin and sent it flying through the air. The dead, skinless horse fell through the roof of the house of Amaterasu. Amaterasu was so terrified that she ran out of the house and into a nearby cave, and pulled a boulder across the entrance. This plunged the world into darkness, causing the very first eclipse!

Who believed that a dragon ate the Sun?

THIS IS PART OF A CHINESE ACCOUNT OF TWO IMPERIAL ASTRONOMERS, Hsi and Hso. One day a giant dragon took a bite out of the Sun. It took another bite, and only half the Sun was left. Then it bit the rest of the Sun. Only a black circle was left with a strange white glow around it. The emperor and people of China were terrified. They did all they could to frighten the dragon. This worked, and the Sun slowly came out of the dragon's mouth. But the emperor was furious that his astronomers Hsi and Hso had not warned him about this event. So he chopped off their heads! This may be the earliest record of any eclipse, although it's not very scientific. It probably happened in the year 2134 or 2126 BC.

Astronomers Hsi and Hso are brought before the Chinese emperor.

Who thought the Earth, Moon, Sun and stars all revolved around a giant fire?
Philolaus, a follower of the great mathematician Pythagoras of Ancient Greece. His idea was that the Sun, Moon, Earth and other planets went around a giant fire that was hidden by another Earth, like an "anti-Earth", black and invisible in space directly opposite us. This was an interesting suggestion for the time, since most people believed that the Earth was the centre of everything and did not move at all.

Why do some people get into water up to their necks, to make the eclipse pass?
Some people in India do this to make sure a solar eclipse finishes and the Sun comes out again. Immersing yourself in water is an act of worship to the Sun and Moon. It supports and helps them in their battle against the great dragon of darkness that is trying to eat the Sun.

Why do some people in Japan cover their ponds and wells during an eclipse?
This custom probably began from the ancient belief that a cosmic dragon tries to eat the Sun during an eclipse. As the sky darkens in the eclipse, the dragon could spit and drip evil and poison onto the Earth. So wells and ponds are covered up to repel the poison and keep the water clean.

Who thinks that during an eclipse, the Sun and Moon gods are checking up on us?
This is a belief of some people in the far north, such as Inuits, Aleuts and Tlingit Indians. During an eclipse the Sun and Moon get together and come down from their normal places in the sky. They check up that everything is OK and people are behaving themselves here on Earth.

How did an eclipse help Columbus?

ON HIS FOURTH VOYAGE TO THE NEW WORLD OF THE AMERICAS (1502–04), Christopher Columbus and his crew were stranded on the island of Jamaica when their ship fell apart. They managed to trade with the islanders for food, but soon they had nothing left to swap. Then Columbus saw in his star charts and tables that a lunar eclipse was due on 29 February 1504. He fixed a meeting with the islanders, and said that his God was angry and would cover over the Moon. The eclipse took place, the islanders became very frightened, and agreed to feed and be nice to Columbus and his men once more.

When did people go back to bed during an eclipse?

During the eclipse of 14 May 1230 AD, in medieval Western Europe. This total eclipse blotted out the Sun for about five minutes. The historian Roger of Wendover described how workers thought evening had come early, so they went home and prepared for bed. To their amazement, since they knew little about science or eclipses, after about an hour the Sun shone brightly again.

Christopher Columbus used an eclipse to persuade the islanders of Jamaica to feed him and his crew.

How did studying an eclipse cause a revolution in science?

Almost since the beginning of history, most people believed that the Earth was the centre of everything. They thought it stayed still while the Sun, Moon and stars went around it. But Polish astronomer Nicolaus Copernicus (1473–1543) had doubts. He realized that the movements of the Sun, Moon and stars could be explained much more easily if the Earth went around the Sun, not the other way round. His calculations of the way the Sun and Moon behaved during an eclipse helped to convince him.

Which emperor was scared to death by an eclipse?

Emperor Louis I of France and the Frankish Empire. He was the son of one of the most famous rulers in history, Charlemagne. Louis controlled the Frankish Empire from AD 814 until 840. On 5 May 840, Louis was amazed and awestruck by an eclipse. In fact, he was so affected that he felt faint, began to worry and despair, took to his bed, and soon died.

How did antique collectors in Baghdad, Iraq, help to save ancient records of eclipses?

In Baghdad in the 19th century, local people were looking through ancient ruins for bricks to build their houses. They noticed some clay slabs had squiggles and lines on them, like writing, and thought they could be valuable. They sold the slabs to antique collectors in Baghdad. The slabs were clay tablets from Ancient Babylon, and the squiggles were a form of writing about all kinds of historical events – including eclipses. They are now kept in the British Museum, London.

Do eclipses cause earthquakes?

NO. MANY PEOPLE HAVE TRIED TO LINK ECLIPSES TO EARTHQUAKES, SAYING that one caused the other. By the laws of chance, an earthquake and an eclipse sometimes happen near each other, even on the same day. But this is just coincidence.

Which King was frightened away by an eclipse?
King Hakon IV of Norway. He sailed with his troops from Bergen to Scotland to punish the king there. As he landed in the Orkney Islands, the Sun faded to become a thin ring around a darker central area. Hakon became frightened and thought better of his mission. Modern calculations show that there was an eclipse around that time. We now know that it was on 5 August 1263, at about 1 pm.

The path of a total solar eclipse

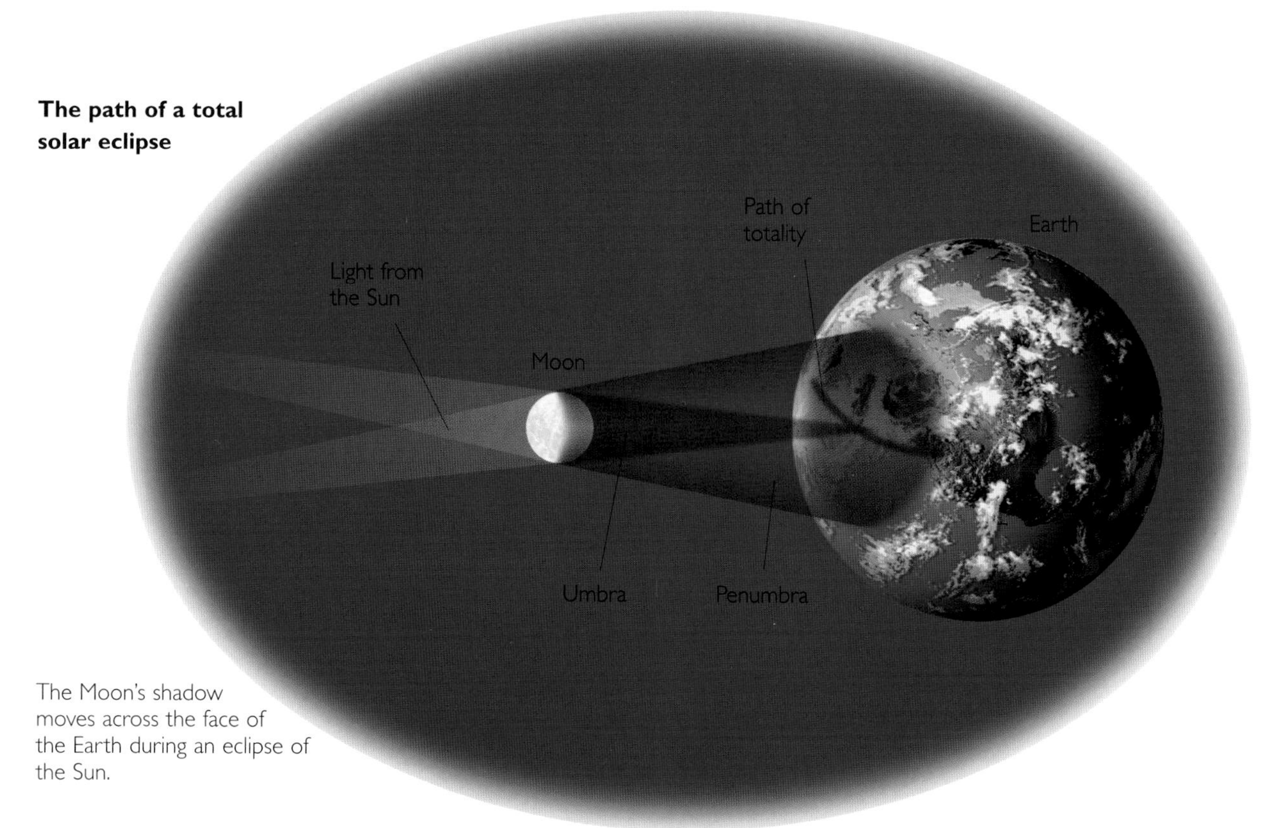

The Moon's shadow moves across the face of the Earth during an eclipse of the Sun.

How wide is the path of a solar eclipse?

THE ROUND BLACK SHADOW OR UMBRA THAT THE MOON CASTS ON THE Earth, during a total solar eclipse, can be up to 268.7 km (167 miles) across. This is its maximum width, and it occurs when the Earth is nearest to the Moon and the Moon is farthest from the Sun. Usually the shadow is narrower than this. Inside this shadow, you see a total solar eclipse.

How long is the Sun totally covered?
In theory, the maximum time for the totality period is about 7 minutes 31 seconds. But this is only when the Sun, Moon and Earth are exactly in line, which is known as precise syzygy! This only happens every few thousand years. There was a totality of 7 minutes 8 seconds near the Philippines in June 1955, but it was cloudy! Usually, the period of totality is around 3 minutes.

How much of the Earth experiences a total eclipse?
The area of the Earth's surface covered by the long, narrow path of totality is only about one half of a per cent – around one two-hundredth of the planet's surface. This is about 2.5 million sq km (0.96 million sq miles). The total solar eclipse track often passes across remote areas such as deserts and mountains, or the sea, so few people see the total eclipse.

How long is the path of a solar eclipse?
The Moon's dark shadow, which brings a total solar eclipse, can cover a path or track up to 9,000 km (5,600 miles) long.

Which way does a solar eclipse move around the Earth?
The round, black shadow of a total solar eclipse moves from west to east for example, from North America across the Atlantic to Europe.

How many eclipses were there in the 20th century?
There were 228 solar eclipses over the hundred years from 1900 to 1999 (including the one of 11 August 1999) and 147 lunar eclipses. This makes a total of 375 eclipses for the century.

Can you see a solar eclipse from an aeroplane?
Yes, you can see a version of it. If it's a total eclipse on the ground, and you are very high up, you may not see the totality because you are seeing it from a different angle. But you may see the Moon's shadow, racing over the ground below.

How fast does the solar eclipse shadow go?

PART OF THE MOVEMENT OF THE MOON'S SHADOW ACROSS THE Earth is due to the Moon going around the Earth on its orbit. But part is due to the Earth spinning around on its axis, once every 24 hours. The speed of the total eclipse shadow is one minus the other. At the middle of the Earth, on the equator, the surface moves fastest and the Moon's shadow travels at about 1,700 kph (1,050 mph). Near the poles the Earth's surface goes much slower and so the shadow moves faster, almost 3,400 kph (2,113 mph).

Where's the best place to live, to see most eclipses?

If you could live for about 350 years in the same place, you'd probably see a total solar eclipse. But this is a very broad average. Some places do not experience a total solar eclipse for thousands of years. Others have them more often – such as a small area of Kazakhstan in Asia, just east of the Aral Sea. People here saw three total solar eclipses in eleven years, in September 1941, July 1945 and February 1952. Any place on Earth should see some kind of partial solar eclipse every two to three years. On average, of course.

How long can a total solar eclipse last?

About two hours is the usual time, with the period of totality in the middle.

The Moon's shadow moves at different speeds, depending on which part of the Earth it falls on.

A bird's-eye view of the Moon's shadow

How long is it from the beginning of a total eclipse, to the totality?
About one hour. The whole total solar eclipse usually lasts about two hours, from when the Moon starts to creep across the face of the Sun from the west side, to when it finally leaves on the east side, and the Sun is uncovered again. The total eclipse part, when the Sun is completely covered, usually lasts about three minutes in the middle of these two hours.

What is emersion?
It is when a total solar eclipse is just finishing. Like the start of totality, called immersion, the eclipse ends with a diamond ring effect as the first rays of the Sun peep around the Moon. Brilliant points of light, Baily's beads, can also be seen.

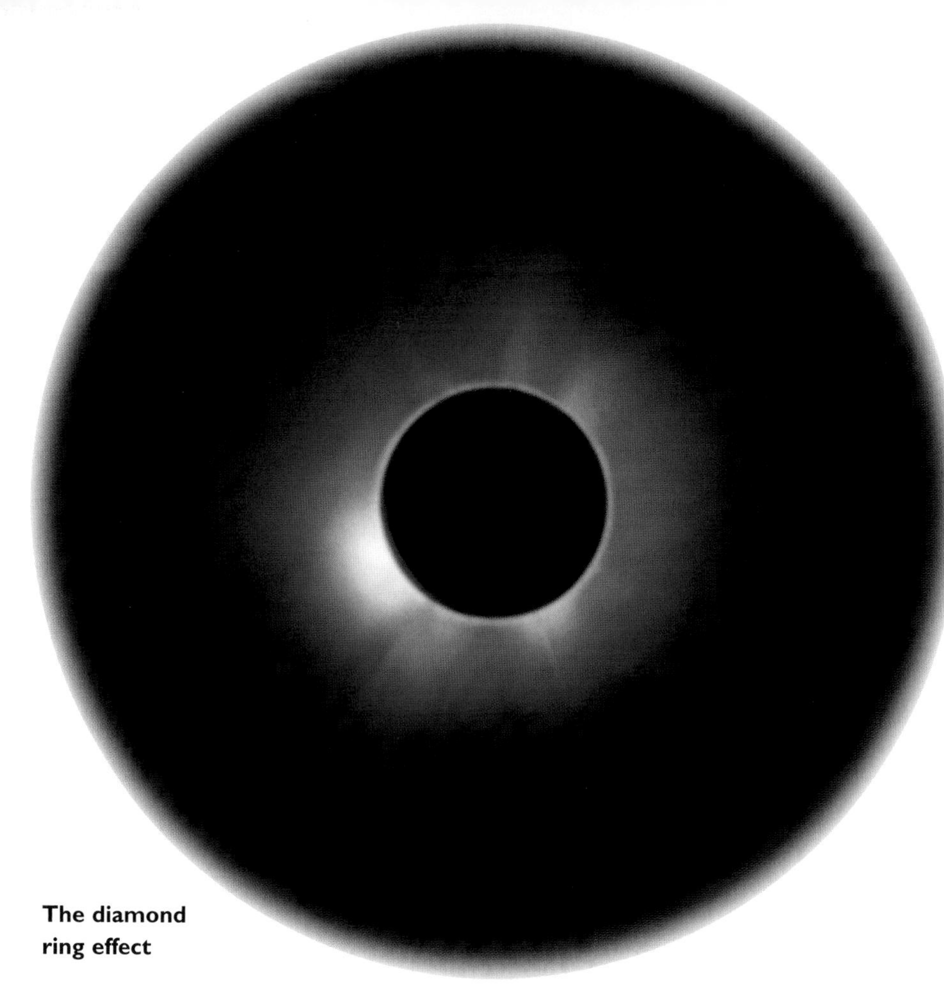

The diamond ring effect

What is the diamond ring effect?

AS A TOTAL SOLAR ECLIPSE HAPPENS, THE MOON COVERS UP MOST OF THE SUN, from the west side. Near the time of totality it leaves just one spot of the Sun on the other side, which still glows with its incredible brightness, like a sparkling diamond. Around the Moon, the outermost layers of the Sun (mainly the chromosphere) glow in a partial ring shape. The whole effect looks like a diamond ring.

What are solar streamers?
These are two long, wispy parts of the Sun's corona that seem to extend sideways, like two long, thin wings. They are best seen during a total solar eclipse. The solar streamers are most obvious when the Sun's cycle of magnetism reduces the corona to its smallest size. They could have inspired ancient people to imagine the Sun as a great being with wings, like an angel.

Why does the Sun's corona vary over the years?
The Sun's faint outermost "halo", the corona, is visible during a total eclipse. It is bigger at some times than at others. This is because the Sun, like the Earth, has its own magnetic field. The changes in the corona are due mainly to variations in the Sun's intense magnetism. These happen over a repeating period of about 11 years and also affect sunspots. As the magnetic field gets stronger, it pulls the wispy gases and matter of the corona inwards towards the surface. As the field fades for a time, the corona extends further into space.

Who took a great photo of a diamond ring in space?
The astronauts of Apollo 12, who went to the Moon in November 1969. They were the second Apollo crew to land on the Moon. Their photograph shows an amazing diamond ring effect. But it was not a solar eclipse. It was caused by the Earth eclipsing the Sun, so it was a lunar eclipse.

What are shadow bands?

These are narrow bands of shadows, like a shadowy version of bars on a jail cell or light shining through a picket fence. You can see them best on large, flat, light, plain-colour surfaces such as the whitewashed wall of a house or a large light-coloured patio. They are often at an angle and they wave or undulate like ripples on a pond. It's not quite known how shadow bands occur. They may be due to the refraction or bending of light as it comes through the Earth's atmosphere.

Shadow bands on the walls of houses

What are Baily's beads?

AS A TOTAL ECLIPSE PROGRESSES, IT BECOMES ALMOST TIME FOR totality – when the Moon covers the entire Sun. Just as the last part of the Sun's blinding disc passes behind the Moon, the last curved part of the disc seems to become broken into a series of bright spots. These vary in size and brightness and have dark irregular gaps between them. They appear up to about 10 seconds before totality. They look like shiny pearls on a necklace or a string of glowing beads – Baily's beads.

How are Baily's beads caused?

As the Moon almost covers the Sun, the Sun's light rays just touch or graze past the Moon's surface. This surface is not flat. It is covered with mountains, valleys, craters and canyons. The last of the Sun's rays can pass only through the valleys and canyons, not through the mountains between them. These rays shine onwards to Earth, where they appear as a series of bright spots – called Baily's beads. They were first explained by Francis Baily, a British astronomer, in the 19th century.

Rays of light from the Sun pass through valleys and canyons on the Moon's surface but are blocked by mountains.

How Baily's beads are caused

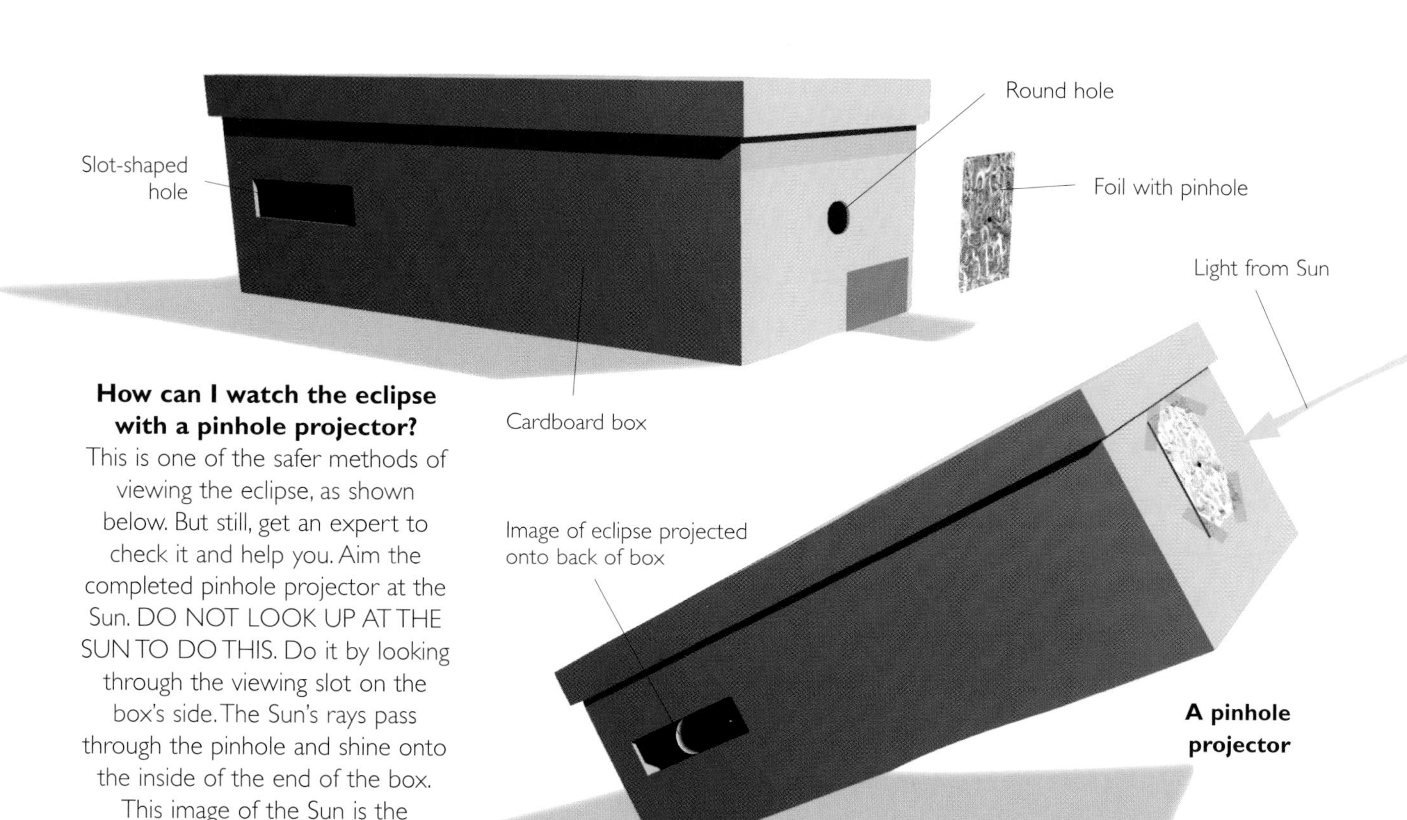

A pinhole projector

How can I watch the eclipse with a pinhole projector?
This is one of the safer methods of viewing the eclipse, as shown below. But still, get an expert to check it and help you. Aim the completed pinhole projector at the Sun. DO NOT LOOK UP AT THE SUN TO DO THIS. Do it by looking through the viewing slot on the box's side. The Sun's rays pass through the pinhole and shine onto the inside of the end of the box. This image of the Sun is the one to watch.

How can I watch an eclipse SAFELY?
The only safe way of observing an eclipse is to do it under the supervision of an expert who knows all about the viewing methods. Follow the instructions and don't mess about, flash mirrors or lenses around, or glance up at or near the Sun. Otherwise the eclipse could be the last thing you ever see.

When do people damage their eyes trying to watch eclipses?
During almost every solar eclipse, someone, somewhere does not know the safety rules or ignores them. He or she suffers eyesight damage, and temporary or even permanent blindness.

How can I see shadow bands?
If there is no nearby flat, light-coloured surface to watch for shadow bands (see page 23), make your own. It can be a bed sheet, towel, sheet of wood or similar. Lay it in a clearing, if possible angled at the Sun. Watch for shadow bands a few minutes either side of totality.

What do I need to make a pinhole projector?
You need a large cardboard box, shaped like a shoe-box but two or three times larger. At one end, cut a small central hole about the size of a large coin. Over this, tape a piece of cooking foil (aluminium foil) so that no light can get through. Then make a tiny hole with a pin in the middle of the foil. Along one side near the other end, cut a slot-shaped hole about 2–3 by 10–12 centimetres (about 1 by 4 inches), for viewing.

Can watching an eclipse be dangerous?

YES IT CAN! NEVER EVER LOOK AT THE SUN DIRECTLY, OR WHILE SHADING your eyes, or peer at it through ordinary dark glasses or sunglasses, or tinted binoculars or telescope, or in any other way, even during an eclipse. In the partial phase of an eclipse, the Sun may seem less bright. But it's still easily powerful enough to ruin eyesight. Never even glance at the Sun. Its bright rays burn the delicate insides of the eyes without pain or warning. You could go blind before you realize what's happened.

How can I make a model eclipse?

YOU CAN MAKE A MODEL OF AN ECLIPSE WITH A FEW EVERYDAY OBJECTS:

- A fairly powerful torch gives the Sun's light rays. For best results this should have a narrow, focused beam, like a small spotlight.
- A smaller ball-shaped object like a grapefruit or large orange is the "Moon".
- A larger spherical object such as a soccer ball or balloon is the "Earth". The "Earth" should be about four times wider (in diameter) than the "Moon".

In a darkened room, shine your "Sun" onto your "Moon" and "Earth".

Where should I go to see an eclipse best?

If you can't travel to the very best site for an eclipse, you could make the best of your local area. Look at a detailed map of the eclipse to see where it will be total or partial, and if partial, by how much (percentage of Sun covered). Know how high and in which direction the Sun will be, at the time of the eclipse. Make sure it won't be hidden behind tall buildings, trees or hills. Visit possible sites a few days before, to make sure. A site on a hill or on a tall building may give a good view of the Moon's shadow coming towards you, as totality almost begins. However in certain weather, clouds form on hills, mountains and ridges. These could obstruct the view. You can get details of the weather forecast from the local weather office. Take advice from local experts or join a guided group. Experts should know the best sites and how to watch the eclipse safely. They should also point out events as they happen during the eclipse. You don't want to miss the tiniest detail. If possible, be ready to move before the event. If you're in a valley and a mist comes down, it's time to head for the hills!

Is my home-made eclipse really a scale model?

It's difficult to get the Earth and Moon far enough apart, to be accurate in your scale model. If your Earth is a soccer ball, then your Moon, in proportion, should be a tennis ball about 7 m (23 ft) away. And your torch, as the Sun, should be 2.7 km (1.7 miles) away, probably halfway to the next town!

Try moving your "Moon" and "Earth" to copy what happens in a real eclipse.

A model eclipse

How did eclipses help Albert Einstein?

How the Sun's gravity bends light from distant stars

Part of the night sky as it normally appears.

EINSTEIN'S THEORIES OF RELATIVITY ARE SOME OF THE MOST important ideas in the whole of science. Albert came up with the theory of general relativity in about 1915. It predicted all kinds of amazing things, including that space can be warped or curved by the gigantic pull of a star's gravity. This meant, as light rays from more distant stars went past the star, they would pass through curved space, and so curve themselves. Now, our Sun is a star. During a total eclipse, you can see distant stars almost next to the Sun. If you could show that their light rays bend as they go past the Sun, this would support the theory. Einstein's theory was tested and proved correct during solar eclipses in 1919 and 1922.

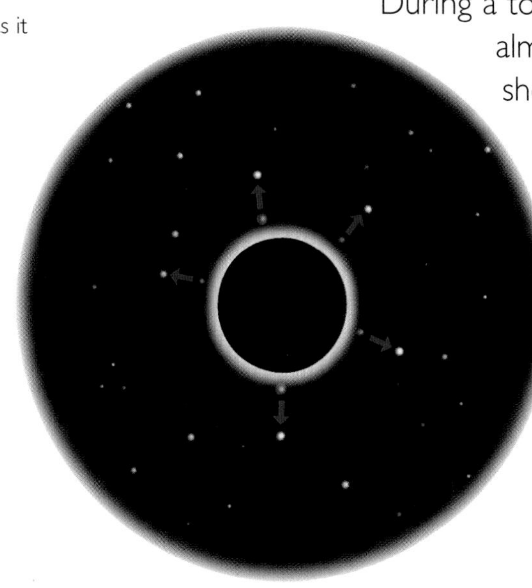

The same patch of sky during a solar eclipse. The Sun's gravity has bent the light from the stars, so they appear to have moved outwards.

Which famous chemist flew alone in a balloon to study an eclipse?

The Russian scientist Dmitry Mendeleyev. In 1887, he floated alone and high in a balloon, to study a solar eclipse. Mendeleyev is famous for working out the chart-like list of all chemical substances or elements, called the periodic table of elements.

Can eclipses tell us that time goes faster or slower?

Yes. The eclipse of 1919 supported Einstein's theories. These also say that only one thing in the entire Universe is constant – the speed of light. Everything else is relative, or varies. This includes time. It can speed up or slow down. As you move faster, time goes slower. If you zoomed to Mars and back, on a journey lasting almost two years, you'd be a few minutes younger when you got back to Earth, compared to if you'd stayed here!

How did eclipses show that light has a speed?

For centuries, people believed that light went from one place to another instantly, in no time. In 1675, Danish astronomer Ole Christensen Romer was studying the eclipses of the moons of the giant planet Jupiter. He was trying to make tables or charts to predict when they will happen. He noticed these eclipses happened slightly later than predicted when Earth and Jupiter were moving away from each other in their orbits. And they were slightly earlier when Earth and Jupiter were moving towards each other. He realized that this was due to light having a finite or limited speed – the first suggestion of this idea.

The Sun

Eclipses have helped astronomers to study the Sun and work out what it may look like inside.

Can you see solar flares better during an eclipse?
Solar flares are huge flashes of flame shooting up from the surface of the Sun. They leap thousands of km into space and usually last just a few minutes. Solar prominences are even bigger, like vast flames licking hundreds of thousands of kilometres into space. They often loop back down to the Sun's surface, dragged back by its intense magnetism. Both solar flares and solar prominences can be seen and studied better during an eclipse.

What do eclipses tell us about the Sun?

DURING A TOTAL SOLAR ECLIPSE, THE SUN'S CORONA BECOMES VISIBLE. This is the faint, pearly-white outermost layer of glowing gases. The next layer inwards is the chromosphere, a thicker, darker layer of the Sun's atmosphere, which glows pink. Below this is the Sun's intensely shining surface – the photosphere, the part we see from Earth as a blindingly bright disc. Normally we cannot make out the corona or chromosphere. They are swamped by the incredible brightness of the photosphere – it is a million times brighter than the corona. But when the photosphere is covered by the Moon, the glow of the chromosphere and the even fainter corona can be seen. Telescopes and other instruments can study these two outer layers of the Sun, and measure their brightness, colours and temperatures.

What is a coronagraph?
It's idea is quite simple. It is a special telescope with a black disc in it, or in front of it, that is just big enough to cover the main disc of the Sun. The disc is called an occulting disc. This is like an artificial eclipse, with the disc being the Moon. The disc can be moved backwards or forwards to cover more or less of the Sun. A coronagraph lets you study the Sun's corona, also the chromosphere, solar prominences and even solar flares.

The Sun's corona

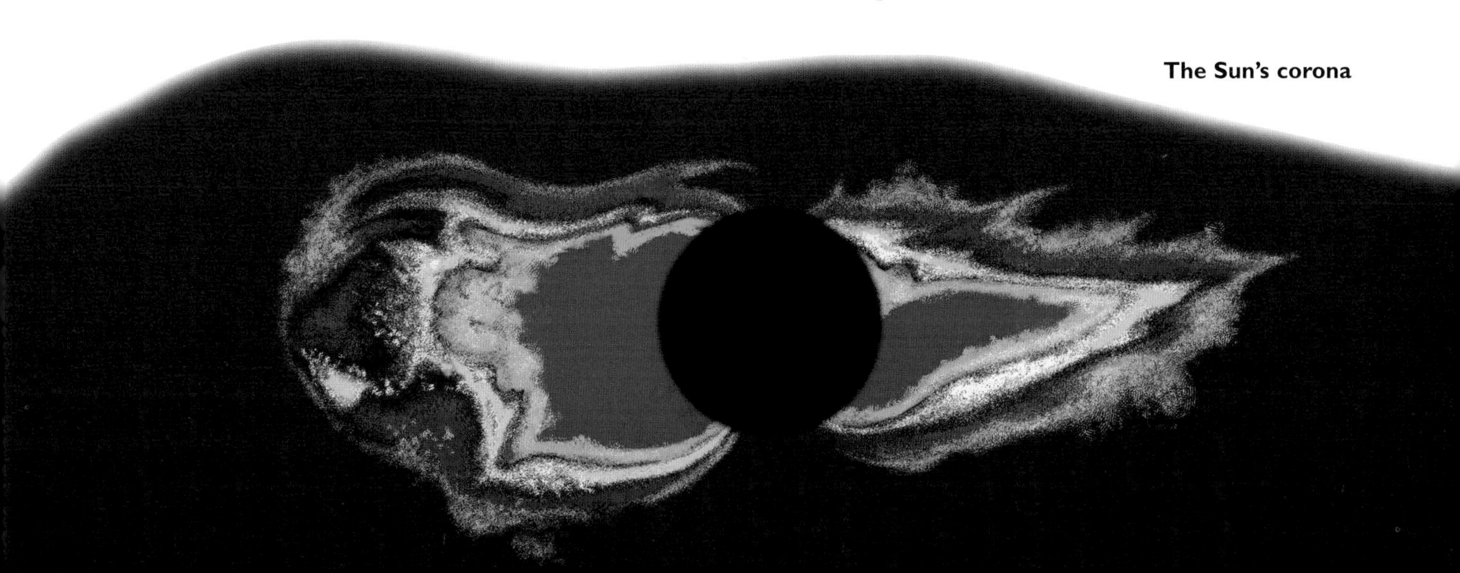

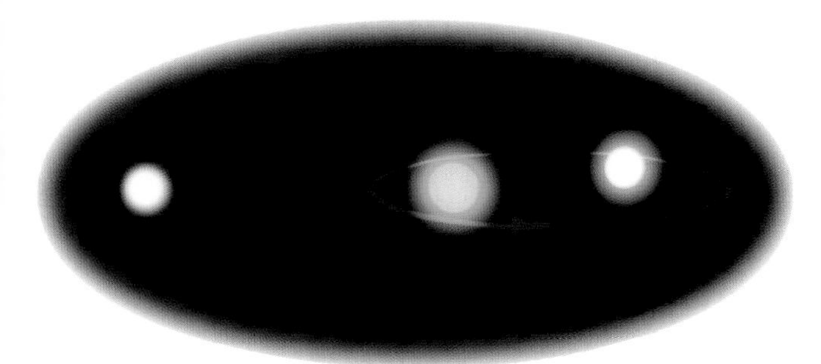

An eclipsing binary star

Why are EBSs called "lighthouses of the Universe"?
Because they seem to flash on and off. This is like a real lighthouse here on Earth, on the coast or at sea. Its flashing warns ships and boats about dangerous rocks and shallows.

1 One of the stars in an eclipsing binary star is normally brighter than the other. When the two stars are close together but not overlapping, they shine with a very bright light (above).

3 When the dimmer star moves in front of the brighter one, the light we see is even less bright (below).

2 When the brighter star moves in front of the dimmer one, the light becomes less bright (above).

What is an EBS, or eclipsing binary star?

A BINARY STAR IS REALLY TWO STARS THAT ARE SO CLOSE TOGETHER they look like one point of light from Earth. They spin or orbit, not around each other, but around the same point between them. Imagine holding hands with two friends, and then whirling them round and round. They are the binary stars, and you are the central point of their orbits. An eclipsing binary star is one which is normally bright, but suddenly fades dimmer for a short time, over a regular cycle.

Why does an EBS eclipse?
We see some binary stars "from the side". The two stars spin so that one crosses in front of the other, as seen from Earth. Normally, we see the rays of the two stars added together to make one bright point of light. But as one crosses, or eclipses, its partner, it blocks out the light from the partner. We see only the front partner's light, so the binary star looks less bright until the eclipse is over. This happens especially when one star is dimmer than the other. Then the front partner goes around to the back, the rear one comes to the front, a similar thing happens, and so on.

How fast can an EBS go dim and bright?
About once every 11 minutes. But this binary star does not shine with light – it gives out X-rays. These are detected on Earth, not by ordinary light telescopes, but by telescopes that pick up other kinds of rays and waves. They are known generally as radio-telescopes. The 11-minute binary may be a pair of very small but unimaginably heavy stars, one white dwarf and one neutron star.

How many EBSs can we see from Earth?
With a reasonable telescope, you can see thousands of stars in the night sky. Of these, about three out of five are EBSs.

How many EBSs are there altogether?
Billions. Besides binary stars, there are also "trinary" stars, where three stars circle each other, and sets of four and probably more. About one-half of all the stars in the Universe are binaries or multiples.

What's the best-known eclipsing binary star?

Probably the best-known EBS is Algol, also known as ß-Persei (beta-Persei). As long ago as 1782, astronomer John Goodricke noticed that every 69 hours, it seemed to go dim for a time, then brighten again. One of the stars in the EBS is brighter than the other, and the dimming that Goodricke saw is due to the less bright partner eclipsing the brighter one.

What do EBSs teach us about stars?

Lots. We can measure their brightness and flashing rates, and also the way their light rays change in colour as they spin round. As one star partner moves away from us, its light becomes slightly redder. This is known as red shift. These changes tell us how far away the stars are and how fast the star partners are moving around each other.

What is the flashing of Algol like?

For about 59 hours Algol stays the same brightness. Then over the next 5 hours it dims to one-third of its normal brightness. Over the next 5 hours it increases back to normal brightness again. The two star partners of Algol are each about 2.5 million km (1.5 million miles) across and 10 million km (6 million miles) apart.

How far away is Algol?

THE ECLIPSING BINARY ALGOL IS ABOUT 115 LIGHT YEARS AWAY. THIS MEANS that light – the fastest thing in the Universe – takes 115 years to reach Earth from Algol. The Sun's light takes only about eight minutes to reach us. So Algol is seven and a half million times farther away than the Sun. It's more than 1,100 trillion km (683 trillion miles) from Earth.

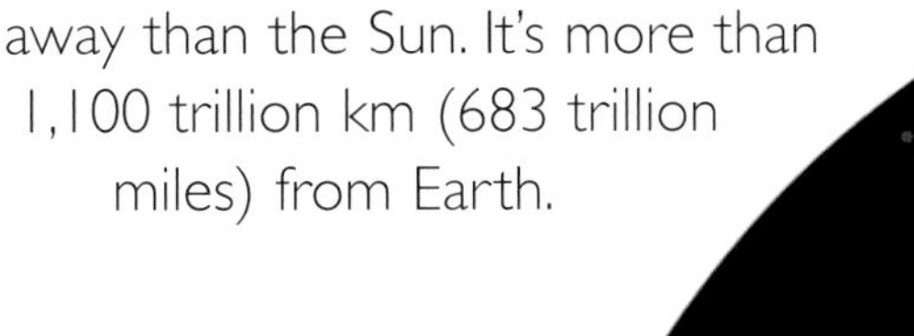

Where is Algol in the sky?

Algol is in the northern constellation or star pattern of Perseus (as shown on the map). Perseus is below Camelopardalis, below left of Cassiopeia, left of Andromeda, right of Auriga and above Taurus. It is like an upside-down 'y'. Algol marks the lowest point of the right-hard arm of the upside-down Y. The brightest star in Perseus is Mirfak, or a-Persei (alpha-Persei).

The position of Algol in the night sky

Cassiopeia
Perseus
Algol
Andromeda
Pegasus
Triangulum
Aries

The eclipsing binary Algol is one of the most famous stars in the sky.

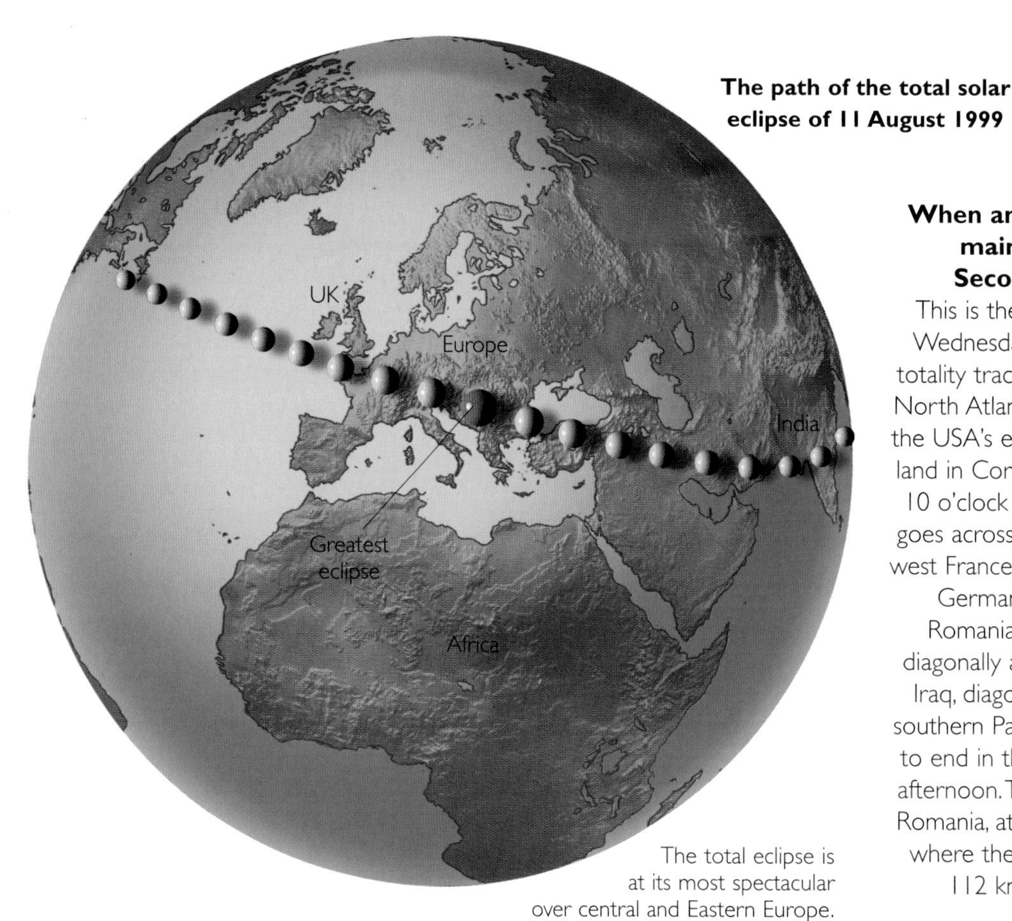

The path of the total solar eclipse of 11 August 1999

The total eclipse is at its most spectacular over central and Eastern Europe.

Which solar eclipse has the most viewers?

THE TOTAL SOLAR ECLIPSE OF 11 AUGUST 1999. THIS IS BECAUSE:

- There are more people than ever on Earth to watch.
- Of these, a higher number know about eclipses, become interested and want to watch them.
- Much of the 11 August eclipse happens over land. Many eclipses happen over the sea where there are just a few sailors and islanders to watch them.
- Also, the 11 August eclipse occurs over very highly populated parts of the world, especially Europe and India.
- We have better communications, with faster news media, loads of television and radio programmes, newspapers and magazines, books and the Internet. The coming of the eclipse has been huge news, giving more people than ever before information about the eclipse.

When and where is the last main eclipse of the Second Millennium?

This is the total solar eclipse of Wednesday 11 August 1999. Its totality track begins in the western North Atlantic Ocean, not far from the USA's east coast. It comes onto land in Cornwall, England, just after 10 o'clock in the morning. It then goes across the Channel to north-west France, across to south-central Germany, Austria, Hungary, Romania, over the Black Sea, diagonally across Turkey, northern Iraq, diagonally across Iran, over southern Pakistan and central India, to end in the Bay of Bengal in the afternoon. The totality is longest in Romania, at 2 minutes 22 seconds, where the eclipse track is about 112 km (70 miles) wide.

Where will the next maximum total eclipse be?

In theory, the totality for a solar eclipse could last up to 7 minutes 31 seconds. This is incredibly rare, happening only once every few thousand years. The closest that we are likely to get to that in the next couple of centuries is 7 minutes 29 seconds. This will be on 16 July 2186. You'd need to be on a ship in the middle of the Atlantic Ocean to see it.

Where will the next total solar eclipse be in Britain?

In an area south of a line stretching from Belfast in Northern Ireland to Dover in Kent. But this is not until 14 June 2151. In London, the eclipse will be 98–99 per cent total.

When will the "midnight sun" be totally eclipsed?

On 1 August 2008, across Greenland and the North Pole, then down through northern Russia to China. At this time of the year the Sun hardly sets in the far north.

Where can we see good eclipses in the future?

THE MAP SHOWS THE MAIN AREAS WHERE TOTAL SOLAR ECLIPSES will be seen until the year 2020. They are spread around most of the world. However the south-east Pacific Ocean is a good place to be. If you had a suitable boat, you could see five total solar eclipses in this region between the years 2005 and 2020.

Where will the next total solar eclipse be in Australia?
On 4 December 2002. The totality path begins in the South Atlantic Ocean, passes over southern Africa and across the Indian Ocean to Australia.

Where will the next total solar eclipse be in the USA?
On 21 August 2017. The totality track will curve from Oregon across and down to South Carolina. The maximum totality time will be 2 minutes 40 seconds.

Can there be a total solar eclipse in the year 2000?
No. The Sun, Moon and Earth do not line up straight enough. So the August 1999 eclipse is the last of the Second Millennium, even if you believe that the millennium does not end until the year 2000. The first total solar eclipse of the Third Millennium is in June 2001 across southern Africa.

What is a "double polar solar"?
This is two solar eclipses that happen at opposite poles of the Earth in the same year. There will be an annular solar eclipse in the Arctic region on 31 May 2003 and a total solar eclipse in the Antarctic on 23 November of the same year.

This map shows where total solar eclipses can be seen. Most of them will only be visible at sea or in the Arctic or Antarctic.

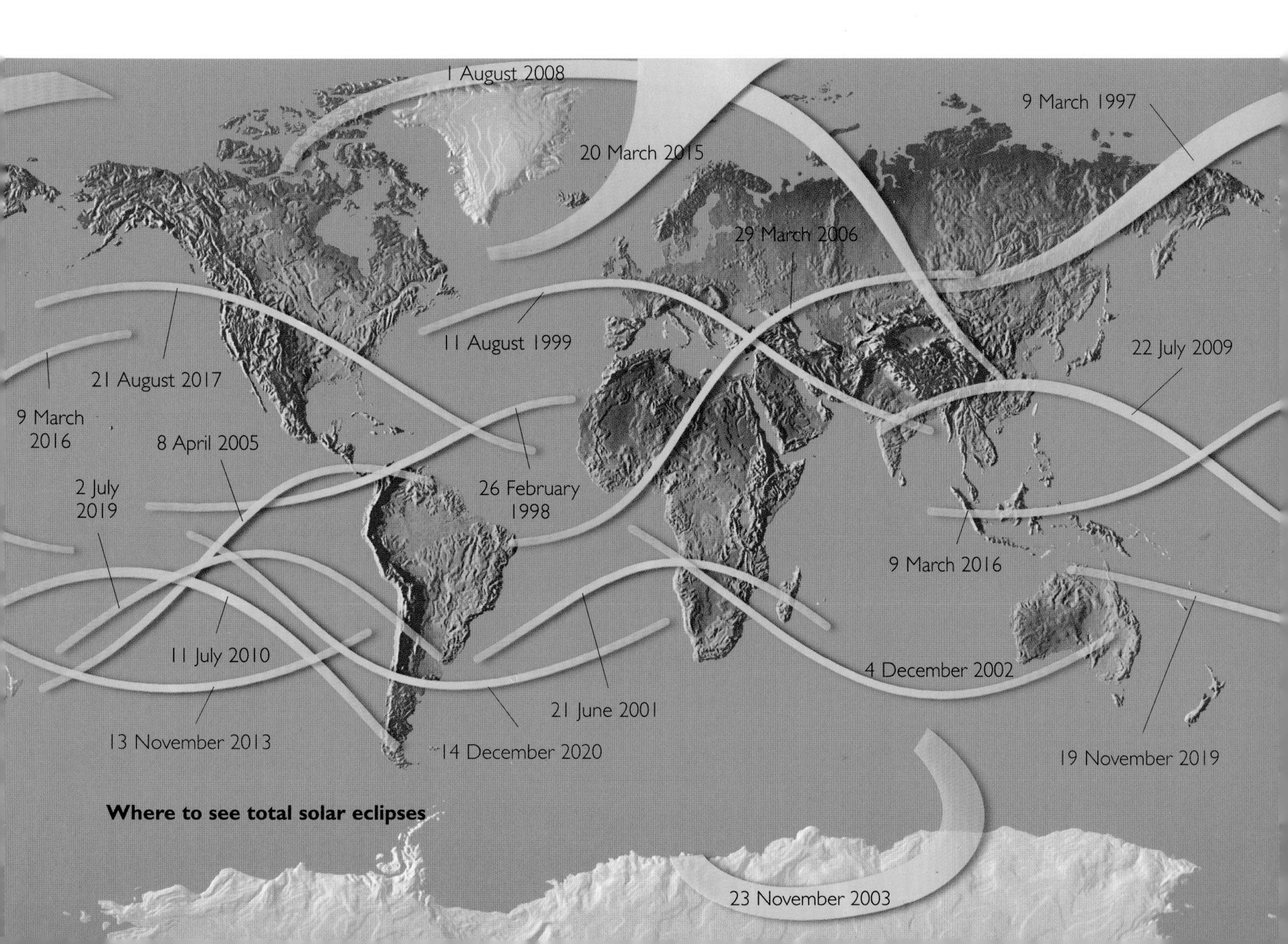

Where to see total solar eclipses

Index